to God for newcomers

Meet Jesus

40 guided Bible readings from Matthew's Gospel

by Jo Swinney

Closer to God for newcomers: Meet Jesus

First published 2012

ISBN 9781844277285

Scripture Union England & Wales
207–209 Queensway, Bletchley, Milton Keynes, MK2 2EB
info@scriptureunion.org.uk
www.scriptureunion.org.uk

British Library Cataloguing-in-Publication Data: a catalogue record for this book is available from the British Library.

Printed in India by Thomson Press India Ltd.

Design by Martin Lore: www.martinlore.co.uk

Scripture Union is an international Christian charity working with churches in more than 130 countries.

Thank you for purchasing this book. Any profits from this book support SU in England and Wales to bring the good news of Jesus Christ to children, young people and families and to enable them to meet God through the Bible and prayer.

Find out more about our work and how you can get involved at:
www.scriptureunion.org.uk (England and Wales)
www.suscotland.org.uk (Scotland)
www.suni.co.uk (Northern Ireland)
www.scriptureunion.org (USA)
www.su.org.au (Australia)

Contents

About the author...

Jo Swinney lives in the south east of England, with her husband, Shawn, and their two little girls. She has a Masters in Christian Studies from Regent College, Vancouver, and a passion for absorbing, grappling with and communicating the Bible. She is the editor of *Closer to God*, and author of four books. She writes for several Christian publications and speaks at churches and conferences as time allows. She will, however, always find time for a chat with a friend over a coffee, and has been known to prioritise novel-reading and playing with her daughters over laundry, washing up and paperwork.

Jo says, 'Having read the Bible my whole life, it has been amazing to try and come at it with fresh eyes. Writing *Closer to God for Newcomers* has made Jesus all the more real to me. As crazy as it sounds, he can be known. I have come to know him better through my work on this project, and my hope and prayer is that you will be able to say the same thing.'

Welcome...

Who is Jesus? Two millennia after his life on earth, literally billions of people claim to know him, and live lives impacted by his teachings. Of the other two-thirds of the world's population, some have never heard of him, some hate him and others are indifferent. What do you think? The best way to clarify your thoughts is to spend time with one of the first accounts of his life.

Matthew's Gospel takes us through the events of Jesus' life, records his teachings, his interactions with his friends, detractors and his Father God, and gives us a window into his thoughts and emotions. It puts him in the context of history and shows how he related to ancient prophecies concerning God's intention to rescue his people. You will be reading words on a page, but these words are living, and through them you will do more than learn about Jesus; you will have the opportunity to meet him for yourself.

The Jesus we will be meeting over the next forty days is a carpenter's son and a king; he is God, and yet he is the ultimate man. He is a fiery preacher and a gentle guide; he is adored and reviled; he died and is alive. This Jesus claims to be God. If he is not, as CS Lewis pointed out, he must be mad or bad. Or could it be that he is what he says he is? This is the most important question in the world. I am glad you have chosen to investigate.

Jo Swinney

Jo Swinney

Introducing...

The Bible

The Bible is the best-selling book of all time and has been translated into over 2,500 languages to date. Literally translated, Bible means 'book' or 'books.' It was written over the course of two thousand years in Hebrew, Aramaic and Greek, by numerous authors. The 66 books that have made it into the Bible as we now know it, are made up of a variety of genres – from historical narrative, to poetry, to prophecy, to letters – and have been available as a collection since AD 405. They are organised into two main sections: The Old Testament, written before Jesus was born and primarily about God's dealings with the Jewish people; and the New Testament, which covers the life of Jesus and the establishment of the Christian church.

However, this is not an ancient, irrelevant, dusty text, but a book so controversial and dangerous that in many countries even today you would risk your life by reading it. It spawns debates, forms national policy, resonates within even the most secular cultural creativity and turns lives upside down. As it says in the letter to the Hebrews, 'The word of God is alive and active. Sharper than any double-edged sword, it penetrates even to dividing soul and spirit, joints and marrow; it judges the thoughts and attitudes of the heart' (4:12).

While the Bible is hugely diverse and spans enormous expanses of time and culture, it has amazing coherence as a whole. It is the story of God's relationship with our world, from its creation, to its fall, to its redemption and its future glory. The central character throughout is Jesus: God incarnate, the Saviour. Christians believe that the Bible is one of the main ways God has revealed himself to us, that the Holy Spirit inspired the many people that wrote it, and that through reading and living by what it says, we will find the way, the truth and the life.

Prayer

If we want to know God, and not just know about him, we need to communicate with him: we need to pray. That is what prayer is: communication with God. It doesn't need special language, it doesn't need to be done in a particular location, it doesn't require training or information. The best way to start praying is to focus your attention on God and tell him what's on your mind.

God's people in the Bible addressed him in many different ways. The Israelite slaves in Egypt cried out to him in desperation, then grumbled at him in the desert, and then worshipped him in the Promised Land. King David adored him, railed against him and poured out the full range of his raw emotions through his psalms. Jesus showed us how to pray to God as our Father, and Paul prayed for everything under the sun. Sometimes it is hard to know how to put our thoughts into words or where to begin, but we don't need to be discouraged by that. Romans 8 verse 26 says 'We do not know what we ought to pray for, but the Spirit himself intercedes for us through wordless groans.'

When we pray, we are not just speaking into thin air – our words go straight to the ear of God. John's vision as recorded in the book of Revelation sees our prayers rising like incense into his presence. And the conversation is not one way – if we listen, we will hear him speak back to us. He speaks through the Bible, through the advice of godly friends, through a persistent feeling or hunch, through dreams, through the natural world, and very occasionally in an audible voice. God wants a relationship with us. He wants us to know him, to be satisfied and fulfilled in him, to love him with all that we are. And the more we pray, the more that will happen.

How to use this book

This book contains 40 excerpts from the Matthew's Gospel, with guided notes on each one to help you understand, engage with and apply what you have read. If you have a Bible, you might want to read the book of Matthew from beginning to end – there's a lot more than we could include here and it will give you a fuller picture of Jesus' life and teachings.

Before you start reading, **take time to be quiet** and ask God to speak to you. Read the opening Bible verse and ask the Holy Spirit to bring the words to life.

Get into the Bible… Read the passage. What's the main point? What is God showing me about himself or about my life? Use the suggestions or questions to prompt reflection.

We have intended to give you the space to ask big questions and to grapple honestly with tricky bits. Grab a pen to jot down thoughts or to underline words or phrases that stand out to you. At the end, there is space to **respond** to what God has shown you through journaling or prayer suggestions.

As you start this book, you might want to pray that the Holy Spirit will bring Matthew's Gospel to life, and that through these words you will get to know Jesus in a real and personal way. This has been the experience of countless people through the ages, and it could be yours.

Mother: human; Father: God

'This is how the birth of Jesus the Messiah came about: his mother Mary was pledged to be married to Joseph, but before they came together, she was found to be pregnant through the Holy Spirit.'
Matthew 1:18

In Matthew's account of the Christmas story, we see things from Joseph's perspective. And perhaps we sympathise with his initial assumption that Mary must have been messing around. The only other conclusion to draw is that GOD got her pregnant...

Read: Matthew 1:18–25

> Joseph is reassured by an angel that his son is indeed Spirit-conceived (v 20). We are asked to accept the truth of this mysterious story too, even as it contradicts everything we know about human reproduction. Can you choose to accept it?
> In the Bible, names carry huge significance. Here we are told two of this special baby's names. 'Jesus' was a popular boy's name at the time and the same as 'Joshua' in Hebrew, who had brought the Israelites into the Promised Land. This Jesus would save his people not just from slavery, but from sin. 'Immanuel', meaning 'God with us', is a theme that Matthew pursues throughout his account of Jesus' life, concluding with his words, 'Surely I am with you always…' (Matthew 28:20).

Consider the idea of God becoming man; the Creator of the universe nestled in Mary's womb. Let it blow your mind.

18 This is how the birth of Jesus the Messiah came about: his
mother Mary was pledged to be married to Joseph, but before they
came together, she was found to be pregnant through the Holy
Spirit. 19 Because Joseph her husband was faithful to the law, and
yet did not want to expose her to public disgrace, he had in mind to
divorce her quietly.
20 But after he had considered this, an angel of the Lord appeared
to him in a dream and said, 'Joseph son of David, do not be afraid
to take Mary home as your wife, because what is conceived in her
is from the Holy Spirit. 21 She will give birth to a son, and you are to
give him the name Jesus, because he will save his people from
their sins.'
22 All this took place to fulfil what the Lord had said through the
prophet: 23 'The virgin will conceive and give birth to a son, and they
will call him Immanuel' (which means 'God with us').
24 When Joseph woke up, he did what the angel of the Lord had
commanded him and took Mary home as his wife. 25 But he did not
consummate their marriage until she gave birth to a son. And he
gave him the name Jesus.

Matthew 1:18–25

Written in the stars

'"Where is the one who has been born king of the Jews? We saw his star when it rose and have come to worship him."'
Matthew 2:2

Read: Matthew 2:1–12

Background info: In the ancient world, events in the sky were commonly held to reflect happenings down below. Scholars have tried hard to work out what this star was – perhaps some kind of supernova, or Halley's Comet. But many think it was most likely the planets of Jupiter (the royal planet) and the planet of Saturn (sometimes thought to represent the Jews) in close conjunction with one another: a new king of the Jews then?

> This new king, news of whose birth threw the current king into such a fluster, was announced in the heavens and worshipped by Magi from the east (v 11). His arrival was a cosmic event – for the Jews, yes, but really for the whole world, for *us*.
> What signs have brought you to worship this king? Reflect on the journey that has brought you to this place.

The magi brought gold, frankincense and myrrh. What will you bring to Jesus?

After Jesus was born in Bethlehem in Judea, during the time
of King Herod, Magi from the east came to Jerusalem 2 and asked,
'Where is the one who has been born king of the Jews? We saw his
star when it rose and have come to worship him.'
3 When King Herod heard this he was disturbed, and all Jerusalem
with him. 4 When he had called together all the people's chief priests
and teachers of the law, he asked them where the Messiah was to
be born. 5 'In Bethlehem in Judea,' they replied, 'for this is what the
prophet has written:
6 '"But you, Bethlehem, in the land of Judah,
  are by no means least among the rulers of Judah;
for out of you will come a ruler
  who will shepherd my people Israel."'
7 Then Herod called the Magi secretly and found out from them the
exact time the star had appeared. 8 He sent them to Bethlehem and
said, 'Go and search carefully for the child. As soon as you find him,
report to me, so that I too may go and worship him.'
9 After they had heard the king, they went on their way, and the star
they had seen when it rose went ahead of them until it stopped over
the place where the child was. 10 When they saw the star, they were
overjoyed. 11 On coming to the house, they saw the child with his
mother Mary, and they bowed down and worshipped him. Then
they opened their treasures and presented him with gifts of gold,
frankincense and myrrh. 12 And having been warned in a dream not
to go back to Herod, they returned to their country by another route.

Matthew 2:1–12

God's way

'Then Jesus came from Galilee to the Jordan to be baptised by John.'
Matthew 3:13

The hype has been growing, the tension mounting. As in Narnia, when rumour has it that Aslan is on the move; could it be the long-awaited Messiah – King, Saviour, holy rescuer – is finally among the Jews? John has announced it, and the stage is set for his appearance. And then, it doesn't go quite as anyone feels it should. Jesus presents himself for baptism; a sign of penitence and repentance. Do you see how upside down this is?

Read: Matthew 3:1,2,13–17

> Why do you think Jesus identifies himself with the people facing judgement and not the God who does the judging? Why is this such a vital symbol for the start of his public ministry, and necessary 'to fulfil all righteousness' (v 15)?
> The Jews would have felt the resonance between their history and the practice of baptism. When the Israelites passed through water they received the Law. Jesus receives the spirit. Baptism remains an important symbol of new life for Christians. Why do you think this is?
> God's unfolding plan to save his people hinges on this man, 'my Son, whom I love' (v 17). In what ways have you been surprised by Jesus? Is he who you thought he was?

'Jesus, thank you for your willingness to be identified with us, to take on our dirtiness and make us clean.'

In those days John the Baptist came, preaching in the
wilderness of Judea [2] and saying, 'Repent, for the kingdom of
heaven has come near.'

13 Then Jesus came from Galilee to the Jordan to be baptised by
John. 14 But John tried to deter him, saying, 'I need to be baptised by
you, and do you come to me?'
15 Jesus replied, 'Let it be so now; it is proper for us to do this to fulfil
all righteousness.' Then John consented.
16 As soon as Jesus was baptised, he went up out of the water.
At that moment heaven was opened, and he saw the Spirit of God
descending like a dove and alighting on him. 17 And a voice from
heaven said, 'This is my Son, whom I love; with him I am
well pleased.'

Matthew 3:1,2;13–17

Temptation

'Then Jesus was led by the Spirit into the wilderness to be tempted by the devil.'
Matthew 4:1

Being a Christian means doing battle with temptation. What do you find particularly hard to resist? That obscenely rich chocolate dessert? The car that's going to make your friends sick with envy? Using the power of your position to halt the career progression of someone you don't like?

Read: Matthew 4:1–11

> Hebrews 4:15 says Jesus knew all temptations known to man. What are the temptations he is faced with here (vs 3,6,8)? Why would they have been particularly difficult for him?
> Why do you think it was important for him to face these temptations as he set out to do the work he'd been called to do?
> Unlike Adam, Jesus resisted the devil. His primary defence was Scripture, and the Word of God is what will help us foil the attempts of the evil one to bring us down. Commit the following to memory:
'If anyone is in Christ, the new creation has come: the old has gone, the new is here! All this is from God, who reconciled us to himself through Christ, ...' (2 Corinthians 5:18).

Thank Jesus that he resisted temptation, that he was the only man ever to remain pure and holy, and was therefore an acceptable sacrifice for our sin.

Then Jesus was led by the Spirit into the wilderness to be
tempted by the devil. 2 After fasting for forty days and forty nights, he
was hungry. 3 The tempter came to him and said, 'If you are the Son
of God, tell these stones to become bread.'
4 Jesus answered, 'It is written: "Man shall not live on bread alone,
but on every word that comes from the mouth of God."'
5 Then the devil took him to the holy city and set him on the highest
point of the temple. 6 'If you are the Son of God,' he said, 'throw
yourself down. For it is written:
'"He will command his angels concerning you,
  and they will lift you up in their hands,
  so that you will not strike your foot against a stone."'
7 Jesus answered him, 'It is also written: "Do not put the Lord your
God to the test."'
8 Again, the devil took him to a very high mountain and showed him
all the kingdoms of the world and their splendour. 9 'All this I will give
you,' he said, 'if you will bow down and worship me.'
10 Jesus said to him, 'Away from me, Satan! For it is written: "Worship
the Lord your God, and serve him only."'
11 Then the devil left him, and angels came and attended him.

Matthew 4:1–11

All or nothing

'"Come, follow me," Jesus said ... At once they left their nets and followed him.'
Matthew 4:19,20

I hated PE at school – I was always the last one picked for the team. If Jesus was captain, I would have been picked first! We all would.

Read: Matthew 4:18–22

> In Jewish culture at the time, a Rabbi – a teacher – would mentor a group of 'disciples', drawn from the elite students of the Torah. Why do you think Jesus chose his inner circle from common fishermen? How do you think they felt to be picked by him?
> Simon and Andrew had no idea what they were committing themselves to, but they must have had an inkling of *who* it was. When Jesus calls to us, do we count the cost, or decide it's worth it whatever?

Imagine: you're at work – work that provides for you, that you know how to do, that your family have done before you. Jesus comes along and calls to you. He wants you to go with him, right then and there. What do you do?

18 As Jesus was walking beside the Sea of Galilee, he saw two
brothers, Simon called Peter and his brother Andrew. They were
casting a net into the lake, for they were fishermen. 19 'Come, follow
me,' Jesus said, 'and I will send you out to fish for people.' 20 At once
they left their nets and followed him.
21 Going on from there, he saw two other brothers, James son
of Zebedee and his brother John. They were in a boat with their
father Zebedee, preparing their nets. Jesus called them, 22 and
immediately they left the boat and their father and followed him.

Matthew 4:18–22

"Come, follow me..."
Matthew 4:19

Upside down is right side up

'"Blessed are the poor in spirit ... those who mourn ... the meek ... those who are persecuted ..."'
Matthew 5:3,4,5,10

Read: Matthew 5:1–12

Matthew's account of Jesus' life is carefully constructed to show us how he fulfilled all the ancient prophecies about a coming Messiah, a Saviour who would usher in God's rule and make things right once and for all. And yet, Jesus continually confounded expectations, reshaping and remoulding their idea of what this Saviour would be like, and the nature of the kingdom he would rule. His teaching here announces a joyful new era, where, under God's reign, the natural order of things would be overturned.

Work through the list below, jotting down your thoughts about how Jesus considers these people to be blessed. Ask him to help you understand the way things work where he is in charge.

> the poor in spirit

> those who mourn

> the meek

> those who hunger and thirst for righteousness

> the merciful

> the pure in heart

> the peacemakers

> those who are persecuted

Now when Jesus saw the crowds, he went up on a
mountainside and sat down. His disciples came to him, 2 and he
began to teach them.

He said:
3 'Blessed are the poor in spirit,
for theirs is the kingdom of heaven.
4 Blessed are those who mourn,
for they will be comforted.
5 Blessed are the meek,
for they will inherit the earth.
6 Blessed are those who hunger and thirst for righteousness,
for they will be filled.
7 Blessed are the merciful,
for they will be shown mercy.
8 Blessed are the pure in heart,
for they will see God.
9 Blessed are the peacemakers,
for they will be called children of God.
10 Blessed are those who are persecuted because of righteousness,
for theirs is the kingdom of heaven.
11 'Blessed are you when people insult you, persecute you and falsely
say all kinds of evil against you because of me. 12 Rejoice and be
glad, because great is your reward in heaven, for in the same way
they persecuted the prophets who were before you.

Matthew 5:1–12

A lesson in praying

'"This, then, is how you should pray ..."'
Matthew 6:9a

If you find praying hard, don't feel bad about that: even Jesus' disciples needed coaching. And here we have the help he gave them: a beautiful framework to help us structure our communication with the God we can approach as 'our Father'.

Read: Matthew 6:7–15

This prayer is not intended to be lifted word for word and used as some kind of incantation. What it does is teach us something about how we can address God:

> Prayer needs to begin with a focus on who we are talking to, otherwise it quickly turns into a self-obsessed monologue. In prayer, we spend time in God's presence and discover more of who he is (vs 9,10).
> We can though, pray for 'our daily bread' – our needs and concerns – because we are talking to the Creator of the world, who loves and cares for what he has made.
> It is always important to pray to be forgiven and for help to forgive (vs 12,14,15). Forgiveness is at the very heart of what it means to be a Christian.
> And we pray for spiritual protection, because we are walking a dangerous and difficult road as followers of Christ (v 13).

Make this prayer your own now. Pray it through slowly, chewing over the meaning of the words as you say them.

7 And when you pray, do not keep on babbling like pagans, for
they think they will be heard because of their many words. 8 Do not
be like them, for your Father knows what you need before you ask
him.
9 'This, then, is how you should pray:
'"Our Father in heaven,
hallowed be your name,
10 your kingdom come,
your will be done,
on earth as it is in heaven.
11 Give us today our daily bread.
12 And forgive us our debts,
as we also have forgiven our debtors.
13 And lead us not into temptation,
but deliver us from the evil one."
14 For if you forgive other people when they sin against you, your
heavenly Father will also forgive you. 15 But if you do not forgive
others their sins, your Father will not forgive your sins.

Matthew 6:7–15

Specks, planks, pearls and pigs

'"So in everything, do to others what you would have them do to you, for this sums up the Law and the Prophets."'
Matthew 7:12

Have you ever heard people refer to Jesus as a 'good moral teacher'? It brings to mind the image of an earnest and scholarly man, holding forth on worthy topics. Well, I would like to suggest to you that the Jesus we meet through the Bible is pretty hilarious!

Read: Matthew 7:1–14

> Picture a man with a plank in his eye trying to 'help' his friend (v 4). How does this image flesh out what Jesus wants to convey about judging others?
> Now imagine chucking a precious piece of jewellery in a pig pen: crazy! (v 6). Jesus was warning his disciples not to try to explain the kingdom of God to non-Jews to whom it would make no sense. After his crucifixion and resurrection, the message would go out to everyone, but for now it was to be treasured and carefully guarded.
> Finally, call to mind a father whose son is hungry and has come running up asking for a sandwich. The dad gives him a rock instead (v 9). Doesn't this jolt us into realising that *of course* God wants to give us good things?

Remembering that God is your loving Father, ask him now for what you need (v 11).

'Do not judge, or you too will be judged. 2 For in the same way
as you judge others, you will be judged, and with the measure you
use, it will be measured to you.
3 'Why do you look at the speck of sawdust in your brother's eye and
pay no attention to the plank in your own eye? 4 How can you say to
your brother, "Let me take the speck out of your eye," when all the
time there is a plank in your own eye? 5 You hypocrite, first take the
plank out of your own eye, and then you will see clearly to remove
the speck from your brother's eye.
6 'Do not give dogs what is sacred; do not throw your pearls to pigs.
If you do, they may trample them under their feet, and turn and tear
you to pieces.

7 'Ask and it will be given to you; seek and you will find; knock and
the door will be opened to you. 8 For everyone who asks receives;
the one who seeks finds; and to the one who knocks, the door will be
opened.
9 'Which of you, if your son asks for bread, will give him a stone? 10
Or if he asks for a fish, will give him a snake? 11 If you, then, though
you are evil, know how to give good gifts to your children, how much
more will your Father in heaven give good gifts to those who ask
him! 12 So in everything, do to others what you would have them do
to you, for this sums up the Law and the Prophets.

13 'Enter through the narrow gate. For wide is the gate and broad is
the road that leads to destruction, and many enter through it. 14 But
small is the gate and narrow the road that leads to life, and only a
few find it.

Matthew 7:1–14

Foundations

'"Therefore everyone who hears these words of mine and puts them into practice is like a wise man who built his house on the rock."'
Matthew 7:24

Read: Matthew 7:24–29

Background info: Matthew has drawn parallels between Jesus and Moses before, and now shows him teaching from a mountain. Ever since Moses received the Law on Mount Sinai, it has been the source of Jewish belief and life. Now Jesus brings a new teaching, and on his listeners' response to his words will their 'houses' stand or fall. Not so far away, the Temple was being rebuilt. Later, Jesus will predict the fall of the Temple (Matthew 24:1,2). Here, he invites his hearers to build their lives on the foundation of his words.

> What words of Jesus have changed your life?
> Are there any that you have held at a distance? Ask him to help you with those teachings you struggle with.

'Jesus, forgive me for the times I have let your words pass over my head. Help me build my life on your foundations. You are my rock. Amen.'

[24] 'Therefore everyone who hears these words of mine and puts them into practice is like a wise man who built his house on the rock. [25] The rain came down, the streams rose, and the winds blew and beat against that house; yet it did not fall, because it had its foundation on the rock. [26] But everyone who hears these words of mine and does not put them into practice is like a foolish man who built his house on sand. [27] The rain came down, the streams rose, and the winds blew and beat against that house, and it fell with a great crash.'

[28] When Jesus had finished saying these things, the crowds were amazed at his teaching, [29] because he taught as one who had authority, and not as their teachers of the law.

Matthew 7:24–29

Jesus heals

'Jesus reached out his hand and touched the man ... Immediately he was cleansed of his leprosy.'
Matthew 8:3

Jesus is in public ministry for three years leading up to his death. Throughout that time, rumours circulate. Could he be the fulfilment of God's promises from the Old Testament of deliverance? Israel has been waiting for a Messiah: someone to save them. Jesus is a powerful and convincing teacher, but could he be more than that?

Read: Matthew 8:1–17

> Do you believe that Jesus can heal today? Have you asked him for healing for yourself or a loved one? Do you know of anyone who has been healed?
> Three years ago, my lovely, faith-filled aunt died of breast cancer in her mid-forties. The kingdom of God has come, but we are still waiting for it to come in its fullest sense. Read Revelation 21:1–4 for a vision of the future.

Spend some time talking to Jesus about those you know who need his healing. Be bold in asking him to make them well. And thank him that his ultimate plan is to wipe every tear from our eyes.

When Jesus came down from the mountainside, large crowds
followed him. 2 A man with leprosy came and knelt before him and
said, 'Lord, if you are willing, you can make me clean.'
3 Jesus reached out his hand and touched the man. 'I am willing,'
he said. 'Be clean!' Immediately he was cleansed of his leprosy.
4 Then Jesus said to him, 'See that you don't tell anyone. But go,
show yourself to the priest and offer the gift Moses commanded, as
a testimony to them.'
5 When Jesus had entered Capernaum, a centurion came to him,
asking for help. 6 'Lord,' he said, 'my servant lies at home paralysed,
suffering terribly.'
7 Jesus said to him, 'Shall I come and heal him?'
8 The centurion replied, 'Lord, I do not deserve to have you come
under my roof. But just say the word, and my servant will be healed.
9 For I myself am a man under authority, with soldiers under me. I tell
this one, "Go," and he goes; and that one, "Come," and he comes.
I say to my servant, "Do this," and he does it.'
10 When Jesus heard this, he was amazed and said to those
following him, 'Truly I tell you, I have not found anyone in Israel with
such great faith. 11 I say to you that many will come from the east
and the west, and will take their places at the feast with Abraham,
Isaac and Jacob in the kingdom of heaven. 12 But the subjects of the
kingdom will be thrown outside, into the darkness, where there will
be weeping and gnashing of teeth.'
13 Then Jesus said to the centurion, 'Go! Let it be done just as you
believed it would.' And his servant was healed at that moment.
14 When Jesus came into Peter's house, he saw Peter's mother-in-law
lying in bed with a fever. 15 He touched her hand and the fever left
her, and she got up and began to wait on him.
16 When evening came, many who were demon-possessed were brought
to him, and he drove out the spirits with a word and healed all who were
ill. 17 This was to fulfil what was spoken through the prophet Isaiah:
'He took up our infirmities
and bore our diseases.'

Matthew 8:1–17

Weather man

'... Then he got up and rebuked the winds and the waves, and it was completely calm. The men were amazed and asked, "What kind of man is this? Even the winds and the waves obey him!"'
Matthew 8:26,27

I am terribly afraid of deep water, and probably one of my worst nightmares would be to get caught in a storm in a small boat at sea. There can be few situations where you are more aware of your powerlessness in the grand scheme of things. But the disciples were OK – they were in a boat with God.

Read: Matthew 8:23–27

> The disciples were spending all day everyday with Jesus, and moment by moment he was expanding their concept of who he was. Now he has demonstrated that he has authority over the very elements of creation. How would you answer their question: 'What kind of man is this?' What have you learnt so far through Matthew about who Jesus is?

'Jesus, you are Lord of all creation, and you are Lord of me. I submit to your awesome authority.'

23 Then he got into the boat and his disciples followed him. 24
Suddenly a furious storm came up on the lake, so that the waves swept
over the boat. But Jesus was sleeping. 25 The disciples went and woke
him, saying, 'Lord, save us! We're going to drown!'
26 He replied, 'You of little faith, why are you so afraid?' Then he got up
and rebuked the winds and the waves, and it was completely calm.
27 The men were amazed and asked, 'What kind of man is this? Even the
winds and the waves obey him!'

Matthew 8:23–27

"What kind of man is this? Even the winds and the waves obey him!"

Matthew 8:27

Authority figure

'"Take heart, son; your sins are forgiven."'
Matthew 9:2b

When I was 6 years old, I stole a pair of sunglasses from a friend. I really liked them, and as we left her house, I sneaked them into my pocket. I have felt bad about it ever since. If I confessed to my sister and asked for her forgiveness, it would make no sense. She was not the person I had wronged. All our sins are wrongs against God however, so when Jesus forgives the man in today's reading, what he is really saying is, 'I am God and your sins are mine to forgive.'

Read: Matthew 9:1–8

> When Jesus looked at the man he didn't only see his physical disability, he saw his sin (v 2). He knew what was going on in the hearts of the other people present too (v 4). Jesus sees everything about us, and chooses to forgive.
> Words can be empty, if there's no substance behind them. Jesus' words brought creation into being (John 1:1–3). They raised a paralysed man from his mat. And they cleansed him of sin. Isaiah 55:11 says, '... my word ... will achieve the purpose for which I sent it.' What have Jesus' words accomplished in your life?

Spend some time confessing the ways you have hurt God lately. Then hear him say, 'Take heart, your sins are forgiven.'

Jesus stepped into a boat, crossed over and came to his own
town. 2 Some men brought to him a paralysed man, lying on a mat.
When Jesus saw their faith, he said to the man, 'Take heart, son;
your sins are forgiven.'
3 At this, some of the teachers of the law said to themselves, 'This
fellow is blaspheming!'
4 Knowing their thoughts, Jesus said, 'Why do you entertain evil
thoughts in your hearts? 5 Which is easier: to say, "Your sins are
forgiven," or to say, "Get up and walk"? 6 But I want you to know that
the Son of Man has authority on earth to forgive sins.' So he said to the
paralysed man, 'Get up, take your mat and go home.' 7 Then the man
got up and went home. 8 When the crowd saw this, they were filled with
awe; and they praised God, who had given such authority to man.

Matthew 9:1–8

A brush with life

'Just then a woman who had been subject to bleeding for twelve years came up behind him and touched the edge of his cloak. She said to herself, "If I only touch his cloak I will be healed."... And the woman was healed at that moment.'
Matthew 9:20,21,22b

As you read this story, try to imagine yourself in the character of the woman Jesus heals. Her condition meant that she was considered unclean, and she would make anyone she touched unclean too. What do you imagine she was thinking as she pushed through the crowds to get to Jesus?

Read: Matthew 9:18–26

> Instead of becoming unclean through her touch, Jesus makes her clean. Take time to fully understand that Jesus has made you clean too.
> Imagine you are in the crowds around Jesus. What can you hear, see, smell? Picture yourself reaching out to touch Jesus. He turns and sees you. What is the expression on his face? What does he say to you? Reflect on this from Isaiah 1:18: '"Come now, let us settle the matter," says the LORD. "Though your sins are like scarlet, they shall be as white as snow."'

'Thank you Jesus that you have made me clean. Thank you that you are the source of all goodness, and that you have brought us forgiveness and new life.'

18 While he was saying this, a synagogue leader came and
knelt before him and said, 'My daughter has just died. But come and
put your hand on her, and she will live.' 19 Jesus got up and went with
him, and so did his disciples.
20 Just then a woman who had been subject to bleeding for twelve
years came up behind him and touched the edge of his cloak. 21 She
said to herself, 'If I only touch his cloak, I will be healed.'
22 Jesus turned and saw her. 'Take heart, daughter,' he said, 'your
faith has healed you.' And the woman was healed at that moment.
23 When Jesus entered the synagogue leader's house and saw the
noisy crowd and the people playing pipes, 24 he said, 'Go away.
The girl is not dead but asleep.' But they laughed at him. 25 After
the crowd had been put outside, he went in and took the girl by the
hand, and she got up.
26 News of this spread through all that region.

Matthew 9:18–26

The heart of it

'"Come to me, all you who are weary and burdened, and I will give you rest. Take my yoke upon you and learn from me, for I am gentle and humble in heart, and you will find rest for your souls."'
Matthew 11:28,29

Read: Matthew 11:25–30

> What does it mean to be a Christian? Some people think it means following a huge array of restrictive rules, or grappling with theological nuances, or contemplating mysteries. Did you ever see it like that? Where did you get that picture from?

> At the heart of Christianity is the invitation to come to God, through his Son Jesus. All that is required of us is a childlike response of acceptance (v 26). Use the journal space below to write your RSVP. How are you going to answer this invitation to come close, to find rest, to learn from a gentle and kind teacher?

'Lord Jesus, I'm sorry that I make it harder than it is. Thank you that you have made it simple to be your follower – not easy as such, but simple, and more rewarding than any other way of living.'

[25] At that time Jesus said, 'I praise you, Father, Lord of heaven and
earth, because you have hidden these things from the wise and learned,
and revealed them to little children. [26] Yes, Father, for this is what you were
pleased to do.
[27] 'All things have been committed to me by my Father. No one knows the
Son except the Father, and no one knows the Father except the Son and
those to whom the Son chooses to reveal him.
[28] 'Come to me, all you who are weary and burdened, and I will give you
rest. [29] Take my yoke upon you and learn from me, for I am gentle and
humble in heart, and you will find rest for your souls. [30] For my yoke is
easy and my burden is light.'

Matthew 11:25–30

The parable of the sower

'"Whoever has ears, let them hear."'
Matthew 13:9

Jesus often taught in stories, called 'parables.' They caught their listeners' attention, but their meaning had to be worked at to become clear, and sometimes Jesus had to spell out what was behind them to his disciples. Matthew has kindly recorded the story and the meaning of it for us in today's reading.

Read: Matthew 13:1–9,18–23

Next to each seed, write the reasons why the seed doesn't grow and flourish. And then consider whether your spiritual health is endangered by that same thing. What can you do to ensure that the message of the kingdom bears fruit in your life?

The seed on the path

The seed on rocky places

The seed among thorns

'Jesus, I have heard your message, through your Word and through the testimony of your followers. Help me understand it, so that I can be like the seed that yields an amazing crop.'

That same day Jesus went out of the house and sat by the lake.
2 Such large crowds gathered round him that he got into a boat
and sat in it, while all the people stood on the shore. 3 Then he told
them many things in parables, saying: 'A farmer went out to sow his
seed. 4 As he was scattering the seed, some fell along the path, and
the birds came and ate it up. 5 Some fell on rocky places, where it
did not have much soil. It sprang up quickly, because the soil was
shallow. 6 But when the sun came up, the plants were scorched, and
they withered because they had no root. 7 Other seed fell among
thorns, which grew up and choked the plants. 8 Still other seed fell
on good soil, where it produced a crop – a hundred, sixty or thirty
times what was sown. 9 Whoever has ears, let them hear.'

18 'Listen then to what the parable of the sower means: 19 when
anyone hears the message about the kingdom and does not
understand it, the evil one comes and snatches away what was
sown in their heart. This is the seed sown along the path. 20 The seed
falling on rocky ground refers to someone who hears the word and
at once receives it with joy. 21 But since they have no root, they last
only a short time. When trouble or persecution comes because of
the word, they quickly fall away. 22 The seed falling among the thorns
refers to someone who hears the word, but the worries of this life
and the deceitfulness of wealth choke the word, making it unfruitful.
23 But the seed falling on good soil refers to someone who hears
the word and understands it. This is the one who produces a crop,
yielding a hundred, sixty or thirty times what was sown.'

Matthew 13:1–9,18–23

Hidden treasure

'"... he ... sold all that he had and bought that field."'
Matthew 13:44

Read: Matthew 13:44–46

Have you heard people say, 'All roads lead up the same mountain'? It is a phrase that implies all truth is equally valid, all religions point to the same God, all of us will end up in the same eternal destination... Jesus says, 'actually there is one truth: Me. And you can have me, but I cost everything you have.'

> In what sense is the kingdom of heaven hidden (v 44)? How did you come to find it?
> What value do you place on your relationship with Jesus? Is there anything you value more? Ask God to reveal to you if there is anything you are holding on to at the expense of living completely in his kingdom.
> We are told that the man in verse 44 went off to sell everything with 'great joy'. What can we learn from that small detail about what it is like to live as a Christian?

'Thank you, Lord God, for showing me the pearl of great price. Help me to see its value, and to invest everything I have in owning it.'

44 'The kingdom of heaven is like treasure hidden in a field. When a
man found it, he hid it again, and then in his joy went and sold all he had
and bought that field.
45 'Again, the kingdom of heaven is like a merchant looking for fine
pearls. 46 When he found one of great value, he went away and sold
everything he had and bought it.

Matthew 13:44–46

'The world and its desires pass away, but whoever does the will of God lives for ever.'

1 John 2:17

A lot from a little

'"We have here only five loaves of bread and two fish," they answered ... They all ate and were satisfied, and the disciples picked up twelve basketfuls of broken pieces that were left over.' Matthew 14:17,20

Jesus has received sad news. Understandably, he wants to be alone, but he can't get away from the crowds. What would you do?

Read: Matthew 14:13–21

Matthew's aim is to build up a picture for his readers of who Jesus is, what he came to do and what response he requires. What does this episode add to the picture?

> Jesus is compassionate. Even deep in his own sadness, he responds to the crowds with great love (v 14).
> Jesus takes the disciples' suggestion and turns it into a seemingly impossible challenge (v 15,16). He likes us to take initiative in responding to need around us, but he will often blow apart our initial ideas and transform them into something extraordinary.
> The disciples do what they can, finding the only food available. Jesus makes it enough (v 20). What do you have to offer – time, money, creativity, passion, a spare room or a talent for catering? Offer it to God, and watch with amazement what he can do with it.

Talk with God about what you have to offer, and ask him to take it and use it to his glory.

13 When Jesus heard what had happened, he withdrew by boat
privately to a solitary place. Hearing of this, the crowds followed
him on foot from the towns. 14 When Jesus landed and saw a large
crowd, he had compassion on them and healed those who were ill.
15 As evening approached, the disciples came to him and said, 'This
is a remote place, and it's already getting late. Send the crowds away,
so that they can go to the villages and buy themselves some food.'
16 Jesus replied, 'They do not need to go away. You give them
something to eat.'
17 'We have here only five loaves of bread and two fish,' they answered.
18 'Bring them here to me,' he said. 19 And he told the people to
sit down on the grass. Taking the five loaves and the two fish and
looking up to heaven, he gave thanks and broke the loaves. Then
he gave them to the disciples, and the disciples gave them to the
people. 20 They all ate and were satisfied, and the disciples picked
up twelve basketfuls of broken pieces that were left over. 21 The
number of those who ate was about five thousand men, besides
women and children.

Matthew 14:13–21

Walking on water

'Shortly before dawn Jesus went out to them, walking on the lake ... "Lord, if it's you ... tell me to come to you on the water." "Come," he said ...'
Matthew 14:25,28,29

Life was never dull for Jesus' disciples. Still reeling from the crazy picnic, they head off across the lake in a high wind only to see someone looming out of the darkness having apparently covered the three or four miles on foot (John 6:19).

Read: Matthew 14:22–33

> Peter was one of the first two disciples that Jesus called, and he came without hesitation, leaving everything behind (Matthew 4:18–20). Why do you think he asks Jesus to confirm who he is by calling him out onto the water (v 28)?

> Put yourself in his place: in the pitch darkness, the wind buffeting the boat and the spray of the waves in your face. Jesus says to you, 'Come!' What do you do?

> I find Peter's courage in stepping onto the water awe-inspiring, but it is somehow also reassuring that he loses his nerve and sinks after a few steps (v 30). Look again at how Jesus responds (v 31). How do you think this episode will impact on the way Peter follows Jesus later on?

Spend some time imagining yourself in this story. See what happens if you are brave enough to get out of the boat.

[22] Immediately Jesus made the disciples get into the boat and
go on ahead of him to the other side, while he dismissed the crowd.
[23] After he had dismissed them, he went up on a mountainside by
himself to pray. Later that night, he was there alone, [24] and the boat
was already a considerable distance from land, buffeted by the
waves because the wind was against it.
[25] Shortly before dawn Jesus went out to them, walking on the lake.
[26] When the disciples saw him walking on the lake, they were terrified.
'It's a ghost,' they said, and cried out in fear.
[27] But Jesus immediately said to them: 'Take courage! It is I.
Don't be afraid.'
[28] 'Lord, if it's you,' Peter replied, 'tell me to come to you on the water.'
[29] 'Come,' he said.
Then Peter got down out of the boat, walked on the water and came
towards Jesus. [30] But when he saw the wind, he was afraid and,
beginning to sink, cried out, 'Lord, save me!'
[31] Immediately Jesus reached out his hand and caught him. 'You of
little faith,' he said, 'why did you doubt?'
[32] And when they climbed into the boat, the wind died down. [33] Then
those who were in the boat worshipped him, saying, 'Truly you are
the Son of God.'

Matthew 14:22–33

Who do you say he is?

'"Who do you say I am?"
Simon Peter answered, "You are the Messiah, the Son of the living God."'
Matthew 16:15b,16

Read Matthew 16:13–17

Who is Jesus? A good moral teacher, a revolutionary who met a violent death, a historical figure who perhaps never even existed? Or the Messiah, the one in whom all God's purposes are fulfilled? This question is at the very core of the meaning of life. How can we find an answer? Let's look at how Peter came to his conclusion:

> Peter was familiar with God's unfolding narrative through history. Again and again Jesus shows himself to be the fulfilment of ancient prophecies. Look for example at Matthew 1:22,23, Matthew 4:13,14 and Matthew 8:17.
> He had spent significant time with Jesus, watching him, learning from him. We can spend time getting to know Jesus through the accounts of his life, like the one Matthew has written. And we can discover what he is like by spending time with people who love him and have become like him.
> We can ask the Holy Spirit to help us understand who Jesus is. Peter's revelation of Jesus' identity came through the Father (v 17).

'Jesus, I say that you are.............'

[13] When Jesus came to the region of Caesarea Philippi, he
asked his disciples, 'Who do people say the Son of Man is?'
[14] They replied, 'Some say John the Baptist; others say Elijah; and
still others, Jeremiah or one of the prophets.'
[15] 'But what about you?' he asked. 'Who do you say I am?'
[16] Simon Peter answered, 'You are the Messiah, the Son of the
living God.'
[17] Jesus replied, 'Blessed are you, Simon son of Jonah, for this was
not revealed to you by flesh and blood, but by my Father in heaven.

Matthew 16:13–17

Cross words

'"For whoever wants to save their life will lose it, but whoever loses their life for me will find it."'
Matthew 16:25

Christianity is sometimes marketed attractively, sugar-coated to make it appeal to the widest possible audience. But we need to know what we are signing up to. Here, Jesus tells it as it is.

Read: Matthew 16:21–28

> Peter doesn't want to hear Jesus talking about his death (v 22). But he has missed a key part of what Jesus is preparing his disciples for: resurrection (v 21). And he misses it right up until he sees, with great surprise, Jesus in the flesh post-resurrection (John 21:7). What Jesus calls us to in following him is what he has modelled – death to self, but ultimately new life.

> 'Deny yourself,' 'take up your cross,' 'lose your life' – these are huge demands. But what are the rewards? You will find life. We mustn't deceive ourselves: following Jesus is costly. It may well cost us everything. But what is the cost of not following him? What in the world could be more valuable?

Use the journal space to reflect on how you feel about this passage:

[21] From that time on Jesus began to explain to his disciples that
he must go to Jerusalem and suffer many things at the hands of the
elders, the chief priests and the teachers of the law, and that he must
be killed and on the third day be raised to life.
[22] Peter took him aside and began to rebuke him. 'Never, Lord!' he
said. 'This shall never happen to you!'
[23] Jesus turned and said to Peter, 'Get behind me, Satan! You are
a stumbling-block to me; you do not have in mind the concerns of
God, but merely human concerns.'
[24] Then Jesus said to his disciples, 'Whoever wants to be my disciple
must deny themselves and take up their cross and follow me. [25] For
whoever wants to save their life will lose it, but whoever loses their
life for me will find it. [26] What good will it be for someone to gain
the whole world, yet forfeit their soul? Or what can anyone give in
exchange for their soul?
[27] For the Son of Man is going to come in his Father's glory with his
angels, and then he will reward each person according to what they
have done.
[28] 'Truly I tell you, some who are standing here will not taste death
before they see the Son of Man coming in his kingdom.'

Matthew 16:21–28

Dazzled

'There he was transfigured before them. His face shone like the sun, and his clothes became as white as the light.'
Matthew 17:2

Today we have yet another facet of Jesus to absorb – the glowing, terrifying, talking-with-dead-people Jesus.

Read: Matthew 17:1–8

> Jesus was conceived by an unmarried teenager, and yet his birth was announced by choirs of angels. He was born in a shed alongside animals, and yet he was there at creation. His closest friends were fishermen and yet he also keeps company with Old Testament legends Moses and Elijah. He burned with holiness and God himself confirmed his identity, and yet he was to be executed as a criminal in naked shame. Take some time to contemplate these paradoxical elements of who Jesus is.

> The disciples' response to the voice from the cloud is to fall to the ground in terror (v 6). This was not an unusual reaction for someone to have in the presence of God. Jesus is 'the image of the invisible God' (Colossians 1:15), but he touches them, tells them to get up and calms their fear (v 7). Have you had an experience of the overpowering presence of God? How did you respond?

'In [Christ Jesus], and through faith in him we may approach God with freedom and confidence.' (Ephesians 3:12). Approach God now with freedom and confidence.

After six days Jesus took with him Peter, James and John the
brother of James, and led them up a high mountain by themselves.
[2] There he was transfigured before them. His face shone like the
sun, and his clothes became as white as the light. [3] Just then there
appeared before them Moses and Elijah, talking with Jesus.
[4] Peter said to Jesus, 'Lord, it is good for us to be here. If you wish,
I will put up three shelters – one for you, one for Moses and one
for Elijah.'
[5] While he was still speaking, a bright cloud covered them, and a
voice from the cloud said, 'This is my Son, whom I love; with him I
am well pleased. Listen to him!'
[6] When the disciples heard this, they fell face down to the ground,
terrified. [7] But Jesus came and touched them. 'Get up,' he said. 'Don't
be afraid.' [8] When they looked up, they saw no one except Jesus.

Matthew 17:1–8

How to be great: God-style

'"... whoever takes the lowly position of this child is the greatest in the kingdom of heaven."'
Matthew 18:4

Jesus must've wanted to knock his disciples' heads together sometimes! They do so well, but then they ask him which of them is most important, a frequent argument. As usual, his answer turns things upside down.

Read: Matthew 18:1–5

> Children were powerless in ancient society. They had no status or privilege other than that of their parents. What was Jesus saying about kingdom greatness when he told them to be like a child?
> The temptation to grab status and power for ourselves is very real. Meditate on Luke 22:26:

'"... The greatest among you should be like the youngest, and the one who rules like the one who serves."'

Ask God to help you seek greatness as he defines it, and not as it is defined by the world.

At that time the disciples came to Jesus and asked, 'Who, then, is the
greatest in the kingdom of heaven?'
2 He called a little child to him, and placed the child among them. 3 And
he said: 'Truly I tell you, unless you change and become like little children,
you will never enter the kingdom of heaven. 4 Therefore, whoever takes
the lowly position of this child is the greatest in the kingdom of heaven.
5 And whoever welcomes one such child in my name welcomes me.

Matthew 18:1–5

"Whoever welcomes one such child in my name welcomes me."

Matthew 18:5

Poor rich man

'Jesus answered, "If you want to be perfect, go, sell your possessions and give to the poor, and you will have treasure in heaven. Then come, follow me." When the young man heard this, he went away sad, because he had great wealth.'
Matthew 19:21,22

Read: Matthew 19:16–26

> Jesus is not pointlessly torturing this young man. He knows that he is a slave to his great wealth, and what he wants for him is freedom. Like the monkey with his hand stuck in a jar because he won't let go of the cookie, the man needs to let go of his possessions before he can truly worship God. What do you need to let go of?
> If you have bought these notes and you know how to read, chances are you are pretty wealthy in world terms. Those who have great wealth have more to lose in truly following Christ (v 23).
> You might think that a camel going through the eye of a needle is a physical impossibility. But 'with God all things are possible' (v 26). Thank Jesus for the eternal life he has won for you.

Jesus said, 'You cannot serve both God and money' (Matthew 6:24). 'Lord, forgive my love of money. Help me to love you more than anything or anyone else, because you deserve my wholehearted worship.'

[16] Just then a man came up to Jesus and asked, 'Teacher, what
good thing must I do to get eternal life?'
[17] 'Why do you ask me about what is good?' Jesus replied.
'There is only One who is good. If you want to enter life, keep the
commandments.'
[18] 'Which ones?' he enquired.
Jesus replied, '"You shall not murder, you shall not commit adultery,
you shall not steal, you shall not give false testimony, [19] honour your
father and mother," and "love your neighbour as yourself."'
[20] 'All these I have kept,' the young man said. 'What do I still lack?'
[21] Jesus answered, 'If you want to be perfect, go, sell your
possessions and give to the poor, and you will have treasure in
heaven. Then come, follow me.'
[22] When the young man heard this, he went away sad, because he
had great wealth.
[23] Then Jesus said to his disciples, 'Truly I tell you, it is hard for
someone who is rich to enter the kingdom of heaven. [24] Again I tell
you, it is easier for a camel to go through the eye of a needle than for
someone who is rich to enter the kingdom of God.'
[25] When the disciples heard this, they were greatly astonished and
asked, 'Who then can be saved?'
[26] Jesus looked at them and said, 'With man this is impossible, but
with God all things are possible.'

Matthew 19:16–26

What I really, really want...

'Two blind men were sitting by the roadside ... Jesus stopped and called them. "What do you want me to do for you?" he asked.'
Matthew 20:30,32

Begging is no one's first choice for how to make a living, but sometimes it is the only way to survive, and a person can get used to managing off handouts. Governments often talk about ways to reduce benefit dependency, don't they? In Jesus' day, an obvious disability such as blindness was a meal ticket, a legitimate reason to live off the generosity of others, so when Jesus asked these two what they wanted from him, the answer wasn't as obvious as you might think.

Read: Matthew 20:29–34

> Do you ever feel that you are shouting to get God's attention; that he is in danger of passing you by, that you sense him somewhere nearby but can't quite see him? Imagine yourself sitting in the dust like the blind men. And then he sees you. You have been noticed. How does that make you feel?

> What do you want from Jesus? Be brave, and ask him in prayer for the thing you most need right now. Use the journal space to note it down.

[29] As Jesus and his disciples were leaving Jericho, a large crowd
followed him. [30] Two blind men were sitting by the roadside, and
when they heard that Jesus was passing by, they shouted, 'Lord, Son
of David, have mercy on us!'
[31] The crowd rebuked them and told them to be quiet, but they
shouted all the louder, 'Lord, Son of David, have mercy on us!'
[32] Jesus stopped and called them. 'What do you want me to do for
you?' he asked.
[33] 'Lord,' they answered, 'we want our sight.'
[34] Jesus had compassion on them and touched their eyes.
Immediately they received their sight and followed him.

Matthew 20:29–34

Hail King!

'A very large crowd spread their cloaks on the road, while others cut branches from the trees and spread them on the road. The crowds ... shouted, "Hosanna to the Son of David!" "Blessed is he who comes in the name of the Lord!"'
Matthew 21:8,9

Read: Matthew 21:1–11

Background info:
> A donkey was commonly used by officials for civil, not military, ceremonies. Jesus' choice of steed signifies that he comes in peace (v 5; Zechariah 9:9).
> Most people of Jesus' time would only have had one cloak. Laying it on the ground was a sign of the highest respect.
> Around 200 years earlier, Judas Maccabaeus entered Jerusalem to the cheers of palm waving crowds, having conquered pagan armies oppressing Israel. Clearly the people had hopes that this was a new king, who would overthrow the Romans; a son of David, Israel's greatest king.
> 'Hosanna' is a Hebrew or Aramaic word, often translated as 'Save us!'
> There was a mismatch between the kind of king the crowds wanted and expected Jesus to be, and the kind of king that he was. What has surprised or challenged you about the Jesus you have come to know through your readings in Matthew so far?

'Jesus help me to recognise you for the king that you are, and give you the honour and respect that you are due.'

As they approached Jerusalem and came to Bethphage on
the Mount of Olives, Jesus sent two disciples, [2] saying to them, 'Go
to the village ahead of you, and at once you will find a donkey tied
there, with her colt by her. Untie them and bring them to me. [3] If
anyone says anything to you, say that the Lord needs them, and he
will send them right away.'
[4] This took place to fulfil what was spoken through the prophet:
[5] 'Say to Daughter Zion,
"See, your king comes to you,
gentle and riding on a donkey,
and on a colt, the foal of a donkey."'
[6] The disciples went and did as Jesus had instructed them. [7] They
brought the donkey and the colt and placed their cloaks on them for
Jesus to sit on. [8] A very large crowd spread their cloaks on the road,
while others cut branches from the trees and spread them on the road. [9]
The crowds that went ahead of him and those that followed shouted,
'Hosanna to the Son of David!'
'Blessed is he who comes in the name of the Lord!'
'Hosanna in the highest heaven!'
[10] When Jesus entered Jerusalem, the whole city was stirred and
asked, 'Who is this?'
[11] The crowds answered, 'This is Jesus, the prophet from Nazareth
in Galilee.'

Matthew 21:1–11

The law of love

"'Love the Lord your God with all your heart and with all your soul and with all your mind.' This is the first and greatest commandment. And the second is like it: 'Love your neighbour as yourself.'"
Matthew 22:37–39

Think of someone you really love: a parent, spouse or child perhaps. Imagine there is a list of rules governing how you act towards them, eg 'Don't eat all their food', 'Talk to them about their day'. You wouldn't *need* these rules: you'd keep them automatically, because you love them.

Read: Matthew 22:34–40

> There were 613 commandments in the Law. Why did Jesus choose these two as the greatest?
> What does it mean for us to love God with heart, soul and mind?
> Sometimes religion is associated with rules and restrictions. How does it change things if you start with love of God and others?
> What is the connection between loving God, loving ourselves and loving others?

Ask God to expand your understanding of his love for you. Let the Spirit speak the truth of his love into the core of who you are.

34 Hearing that Jesus had silenced the Sadducees, the Pharisees
got together. 35 One of them, an expert in the law, tested him with this
question: 36 'Teacher, which is the greatest commandment in the Law?'
37 Jesus replied: '"Love the Lord your God with all your heart and with
all your soul and with all your mind." 38 This is the first and greatest
commandment. 39 And the second is like it: "Love your neighbour
as yourself." 40 All the Law and the Prophets hang on these two
commandments.'

Matthew 22:34–40

'This is love: not that we loved God,
but that he loved us and sent his
Son as an atoning sacrifice for our
sins...since God so loved us, we
ought to love one another.'
1 John 4:10,11

Be prepared

'"At midnight, the cry rang out: 'Here's the bridegroom! Come out to meet him!' Then all the virgins woke up and trimmed their lamps. The foolish ones said to the wise, 'Give us some of your oil, our lamps are going out.'"'
Matthew 25:6–8

Have you ever been caught out by inadequate preparation? Perhaps you've run out of petrol in the middle of nowhere, or been stuck without a spare pen in an exam, or left the house with a baby and forgotten to bring spare nappies…

Read: Matthew 25:1–13

> This is another one of Jesus' 'parables', stories that illustrate a point. Here, he wants his hearers to see how imperative it is that they recognise him for who he is – the Messiah – before it is too late. The Jews had been waiting for him for generations (v 5), but many of them weren't ready to respond when he arrived (v 10).
> We are in a period of waiting again, waiting for Jesus to return: 'When the Son of Man comes in his glory, and all the angels with him, he will sit on his glorious throne … and he will separate the people one from another as a shepherd separates the sheep from the goats' (Matthew 25:31,32). How can we make sure we are ready for him?

'Come, Lord Jesus! I'm ready!'

'At that time the kingdom of heaven will be like ten virgins who
took their lamps and went out to meet the bridegroom. 2 Five of
them were foolish and five were wise. 3 The foolish ones took their
lamps but did not take any oil with them. 4 The wise ones, however,
took oil in jars along with their lamps. 5 The bridegroom was a long
time in coming, and they all became drowsy and fell asleep.
6 'At midnight the cry rang out: "Here's the bridegroom! Come out
to meet him!"
7 'Then all the virgins woke up and trimmed their lamps. 8 The
foolish ones said to the wise, "Give us some of your oil; our lamps
are going out."
9 '"No," they replied, "there may not be enough for both us and you.
Instead, go to those who sell oil and buy some for yourselves."
10 'But while they were on their way to buy the oil, the bridegroom
arrived. The virgins who were ready went in with him to the wedding
banquet. And the door was shut.
11 'Later the others also came. "Lord, Lord," they said, "open the
door for us!"
12 'But he replied, "Truly I tell you, I don't know you."
13 'Therefore keep watch, because you do not know the day or
the hour.

Matthew 25:1–13

Body and blood

'... Jesus took bread ... saying, "Take and eat; this is my body." Then he took a cup, and ... gave it to them, saying, "Drink from it, all of you. This is my blood of the covenant, which is poured out for many for the forgiveness of sins."'
Matthew 26:26–28

Read: Matthew 26:17–29

> The Passover is a Jewish festival commemorating the night that the Israelites escaped slavery in Egypt. An angel passed through the land killing the first-born sons of their oppressors, sparing those who had daubed lamb's blood on the door frame (Exodus 12). Here, Jesus gives new meaning to the familiar symbols of Passover: he is the lamb to be slain for the salvation of many.
> Christians around the world still drink wine and eat bread in remembrance of what Jesus did. As with any ritual, it is easy to lose the impact of its significance with time and familiarity. Allow yourself to be shocked by the words – 'drink my blood,' 'eat my flesh.' The next time you take communion, make a special effort to engage with its meaning.

We might be horrified by Judas' actions, but who hasn't betrayed Jesus in big or small ways? Take time to say sorry to Jesus, and thank him for his faithfulness and mercy: '... while we were still sinners, Christ died for us' (Romans 5:8).

17 On the first day of the Festival of Unleavened Bread, the
disciples came to Jesus and asked, 'Where do you want us to make
preparations for you to eat the Passover?'
18 He replied, 'Go into the city to a certain man and tell him, "The
Teacher says: my appointed time is near. I am going to celebrate the
Passover with my disciples at your house."' 19 So the disciples did as
Jesus had directed them and prepared the Passover.
20 When evening came, Jesus was reclining at the table with the Twelve.
21 And while they were eating, he said, 'Truly I tell you, one of you will
betray me.'
22 They were very sad and began to say to him one after the other,
'Surely you don't mean me, Lord?'
23 Jesus replied, 'The one who has dipped his hand into the bowl
with me will betray me. 24 The Son of Man will go just as it is written
about him. But woe to that man who betrays the Son of Man! It
would be better for him if he had not been born.'
25 Then Judas, the one who would betray him, said, 'Surely you don't
mean me, Rabbi?'
Jesus answered, 'You have said so.'
26 While they were eating, Jesus took bread, and when he had given
thanks, he broke it and gave it to his disciples, saying, 'Take and eat;
this is my body.'
27 Then he took a cup, and when he had given thanks, he gave it
to them, saying, 'Drink from it, all of you. 28 This is my blood of the
covenant, which is poured out for many for the forgiveness of sins. 29
I tell you, I will not drink from this fruit of the vine from now on until
that day when I drink it new with you in my Father's kingdom.'

Matthew 26:17–29

Anguished soul

'"... My soul is overwhelmed with sorrow to the point of death. Stay here and keep watch with me."'
Matthew 26:38

To understand Jesus, we have to grasp both his divinity and his humanity. It is here, in Gethsemane, that we see him at his most vulnerable, facing what is coming and pleading for another way out. He is in under such emotional stress that he sweats blood (Luke 22:44), and he needs his friends. This is not an easy account to read.

Read: Matthew 26:36–46

> Jesus has been to the blackest place a person can go. He has experienced betrayal, sorrow, temptation, desperation, pain – and he knows exactly how you feel at your worst.
> The concept of the Trinity is profoundly mysterious. Somehow, God is Father, Son and Holy Spirit – three separate persons and yet one. It may seem here as though a father is sending his son to a gruesome death (v 39), but we need to remember that the Father and Son are one (John 10:30).
> How does this insight into what this sacrifice cost Jesus affect how you receive the gift of his grace?

Is there a situation in your life when you can see what the right thing to do is but it seems too hard? Ask God for the courage to echo Jesus' words, 'Not as I will, but as you will' (v 39).

36 Then Jesus went with his disciples to a place called
Gethsemane, and he said to them, 'Sit here while I go over there
and pray.' 37 He took Peter and the two sons of Zebedee along with
him, and he began to be sorrowful and troubled. 38 Then he said to
them, 'My soul is overwhelmed with sorrow to the point of death.
Stay here and keep watch with me.'
39 Going a little farther, he fell with his face to the ground and
prayed, 'My Father, if it is possible, may this cup be taken from me.
Yet not as I will, but as you will.'
40 Then he returned to his disciples and found them sleeping.
'Couldn't you men keep watch with me for one hour?' he asked
Peter. 41 'Watch and pray so that you will not fall into temptation. The
spirit is willing, but the flesh is weak.'
42 He went away a second time and prayed, 'My Father, if it is not
possible for this cup to be taken away unless I drink it, may your will
be done.'
43 When he came back, he again found them sleeping, because
their eyes were heavy. 44 So he left them and went away once more
and prayed the third time, saying the same thing.
45 Then he returned to the disciples and said to them, 'Are you still
sleeping and resting? Look, the hour has come, and the Son of Man
is delivered into the hands of sinners. 46 Rise! Let us go! Here comes
my betrayer!'

Matthew 26:36–46

Jesus arrested

"Do you think I cannot call on my Father, and he will at once put at my disposal more than twelve legions of angels? But how then would the Scriptures be fulfilled that say it must happen in this way?"
Matthew 26:53,54

Read: Matthew 26:47–56

Often the truest reflection of our character is how we behave in extremis. Let's look at some clues to Jesus' character in this passage:

> Judas has led an armed crowd to Jesus and identified him with a kiss – a cruel and intimate betrayal. Jesus calls him 'friend' (v 50). Is there anyone in your life who has betrayed you? How do you feel about them now?
> One of Jesus' supporters strikes out in his defence. Luke's account tells us that Jesus heals the severed ear (Luke 22:51). Here, we are told that he knows he could at any point fight back and escape his fate, but he willingly submits (v 53) and defuses the violence. Have you ever chosen not to retaliate? What happened as a result of what you decided to do or not do?
> Jesus knows the Scriptures inside out, and they give him strength, courage and purpose (vs 54,56). Do you find the Bible to be a source of help in dire circumstance?

'Jesus, help me to become more like you as I get to know you.'

47 While he was still speaking, Judas, one of the Twelve, arrived. With him was a large crowd armed with swords and clubs, sent from the chief priests and the elders of the people. 48 Now the betrayer had arranged a signal with them: 'The one I kiss is the man; arrest him.'

49 Going at once to Jesus, Judas said, 'Greetings, Rabbi!' and kissed him.

50 Jesus replied, 'Do what you came for, friend.'

Then the men stepped forward, seized Jesus and arrested him. 51 With that, one of Jesus' companions reached for his sword, drew it out and struck the servant of the high priest, cutting off his ear.

52 'Put your sword back in its place,' Jesus said to him, 'for all who draw the sword will die by the sword. 53 Do you think I cannot call on my Father, and he will at once put at my disposal more than twelve legions of angels? 54 But how then would the Scriptures be fulfilled that say it must happen in this way?'

55 In that hour Jesus said to the crowd, 'Am I leading a rebellion, that you have come out with swords and clubs to capture me? Every day I sat in the temple courts teaching, and you did not arrest me. 56 But this has all taken place that the writings of the prophets might be fulfilled.' Then all the disciples deserted him and fled.

Matthew 26:47–56

Procedural drama

'"I charge you under oath by the living God: Tell us if you are the Messiah, the Son of God."
"You have said so," Jesus replied ...'
Matthew 26:63b,64

Are you a fan of legal dramas? I have been hooked on enough to feel I have a tentative grasp on courtroom procedure, and this trial makes me mad. I object!

Read: Matthew 26:57–68

> The chief priests and the Sanhedrin (the Jewish tribunal) wanted to put Jesus to death, and were looking for reasons to do it (v 59). Why do you think this was?
> Jesus quotes from Daniel 7:13 in verse 64. This is a vision in which 'a son of man' is given authority by the 'Ancient of Days'. Jesus is identifying himself as the Messiah – but Caiaphas disagrees!
> From the glorious image of Jesus sitting at God's right hand in heaven, a different reality is superimposed – Jesus is spat on, beaten, laughed at (v 67). People still mock him. But others recognise his majesty and worship him, following him to death. How about you?

Spend some time reflecting on these two pictures of Jesus, one glorified and exalted, the other beaten and despised. This is our God.

57 Those who had arrested Jesus took him to Caiaphas the high
priest, where the teachers of the law and the elders had assembled.
58 But Peter followed him at a distance, right up to the courtyard of
the high priest. He entered and sat down with the guards to see the
outcome.
59 The chief priests and the whole Sanhedrin were looking for false
evidence against Jesus so that they could put him to death. 60 But
they did not find any, though many false witnesses came forward.
Finally two came forward 61 and declared, 'This fellow said, "I am
able to destroy the temple of God and rebuild it in three days."'
62 Then the high priest stood up and said to Jesus, 'Are you not
going to answer? What is this testimony that these men are bringing
against you?' 63 But Jesus remained silent.
The high priest said to him, 'I charge you under oath by the living
God: Tell us if you are the Messiah, the Son of God.'
64 'You have said so,' Jesus replied. 'But I say to all of you: from now
on you will see the Son of Man sitting at the right hand of the Mighty
One and coming on the clouds of heaven.'
65 Then the high priest tore his clothes and said, 'He has spoken
blasphemy! Why do we need any more witnesses? Look, now you
have heard the blasphemy. 66 What do you think?'
'He is worthy of death,' they answered.
67 Then they spat in his face and struck him with their fists. Others
slapped him 68 and said, 'Prophesy to us, Messiah. Who hit you?'

Matthew 26:57–68

Denial

'Then Peter remembered the word Jesus had spoken: "Before the cock crows, you will disown me three times." And he went outside and wept bitterly.'
Matthew 26:75

Read: Matthew 26:69–75

There are all sorts of ways to cry – softly and sadly, great heaving sobs of self-pity, secretive snuffles, hot, angry tears... Peter, Matthew tells us, 'wept bitterly.' Why?

> Just a few hours earlier, Peter had vowed, 'Even if I have to die with you, I will never disown you' (v 35). Any illusions he had of himself as a man of loyalty, honour, courage, or faith were smashed. He had blown it (v 74). Have you ever let yourself down in a dramatic fashion?
> Jesus had predicted his denials, down to the detail of the cockerel's crow. If Peter needed any more evidence that Jesus was who he said he was, he had it.
> Peter loved Jesus, and knew he was suffering badly. He had wanted to be the one person not to let him down, but he hadn't managed. His friend was all alone, and the knowledge of that was crushing.

We have all let Jesus down at times. Pray for the courage to acknowledge that you are 'one of them', whatever the consequences. Ask God to forgive you for being less than you want to be, and thank him that he loves you anyway.

[69] Now Peter was sitting out in the courtyard, and a servant-girl
came to him. 'You also were with Jesus of Galilee,' she said.
[70] But he denied it before them all. 'I don't know what you're talking
about,' he said.
[71] Then he went out to the gateway, where another servant-girl
saw him and said to the people there, 'This fellow was with Jesus
of Nazareth.'
[72] He denied it again, with an oath: 'I don't know the man!'
[73] After a little while, those standing there went up to Peter and said,
'Surely you are one of them; your accent gives you away.'
[74] Then he began to call down curses, and he swore to them, 'I don't
know the man!'
Immediately a cock crowed. [75] Then Peter remembered the word
Jesus had spoken: 'Before the cock crows, you will disown me three
times.' And he went outside and wept bitterly.

Matthew 26:69–75

Who's to blame?

'"I am innocent of this man's blood," [Pilate] said. "It is your responsibility."
All the people answered, "His blood is on us and on our children!"'
Matthew 27:24b,25

The people demanded Jesus' crucifixion, but Pilate could have overruled them. The chief priests had handed him over in the first place, but Judas had led them to him. Whose fault is it that Jesus was executed?

Read: Matthew 27:11–26

> Barabbas was a 'well-known prisoner', who had been involved in a rebellion, and had committed murder (Mark 15:7). Barabbas gets his life in exchange for Jesus'. How does this detail shed light on the rest of our reading today?
> Do you think Matthew absolves Pilate with the mention of washing his hands? What do you think of his actions?
> We are all implicated in the death of Jesus. Read these words from Isaiah slowly and prayerfully, and try to absorb what the death of Jesus means for all of us:

'Surely he took up our pain and bore our suffering, yet we considered him punished by God, stricken by him, and afflicted. But he was pierced for our transgressions, he was crushed for our iniquities; the punishment that brought us peace was on him, and by his wounds we are healed.' (Isaiah 53:4,5)

[11] Meanwhile Jesus stood before the governor, and the
governor asked him, 'Are you the king of the Jews?'
'You have said so,' Jesus replied.
[12] When he was accused by the chief priests and the elders, he gave
no answer. [13] Then Pilate asked him, 'Don't you hear the testimony
they are bringing against you?' [14] But Jesus made no reply, not even
to a single charge – to the great amazement of the governor.
[15] Now it was the governor's custom at the festival to release a
prisoner chosen by the crowd. [16] At that time they had a well-known
prisoner whose name was Jesus Barabbas. [17] So when the crowd
had gathered, Pilate asked them, 'Which one do you want me to
release to you: Jesus Barabbas, or Jesus who is called the Messiah?'
[18] For he knew it was out of self-interest that they had handed Jesus
over to him.
[19] While Pilate was sitting on the judge's seat, his wife sent him this
message: 'Don't have anything to do with that innocent man, for I
have suffered a great deal today in a dream because of him.'
[20] But the chief priests and the elders persuaded the crowd to ask for
Barabbas and to have Jesus executed.
[21] 'Which of the two do you want me to release to you?' asked
the governor.
'Barabbas,' they answered.
[22] 'What shall I do, then, with Jesus who is called the Messiah?'
Pilate asked.
They all answered, 'Crucify him!'
[23] 'Why? What crime has he committed?' asked Pilate.
But they shouted all the louder, 'Crucify him!'
[24] When Pilate saw that he was getting nowhere, but that instead
an uproar was starting, he took water and washed his hands in front
of the crowd. 'I am innocent of this man's blood,' he said. 'It is
your responsibility!'
[25] All the people answered, 'His blood is on us and on our children!'
[26] Then he released Barabbas to them. But he had Jesus flogged,
and handed him over to be crucified.

Matthew 27:11–26

Royal treatment

'They stripped him and put a scarlet robe on him, and then twisted together a crown of thorns and set it on his head ... Then they knelt in front of him and mocked him ...'
Matthew 27:28,29

Read: Matthew 27:27–31

Background info: Jesus is now in the hands of the Romans, surrounded by up to 600 soldiers. Stationed in an unstable outpost, dealing with repeated insurgency, probably pretty fed up... Here they have opportunity to revel in the might of their emperor by showing just how regal the so-called king of the Jews is.
> The Jews wanted Jesus to be a leader who could deliver them from their political oppressors. It was clear at this moment that this was not what Jesus had come to do.
> This is a brutal account of bullying and torture. What situations are you aware of in the world at the moment where the strong are abusing power? How can you stand up for justice?

'Jesus, you are my king. I kneel before you and worship you now.'

[27] Then the governor's soldiers took Jesus into the Praetorium
and gathered the whole company of soldiers round him. [28] They
stripped him and put a scarlet robe on him, [29] and then twisted
together a crown of thorns and set it on his head. They put a staff
in his right hand. Then they knelt in front of him and mocked him.
'Hail, king of the Jews!' they said. [30] They spat on him, and took the
staff and struck him on the head again and again. [31] After they had
mocked him, they took off the robe and put his own clothes on him.
Then they led him away to crucify him.

Matthew 27:27–31

'Jesus, you are my king...'

Nailed in place

'When they had crucified him, they divided up his clothes by casting lots ... Above his head they placed the written charge against him: THIS IS JESUS, THE KING OF THE JEWS.'
Matthew 27:35,37

Before you read Matthew's account of Jesus' crucifixion, read these words from Psalm 22, written centuries earlier:

'All who see me mock me; they hurl insults, shaking their heads. "He trusts in the LORD," they say, "let the LORD rescue him"... a pack of villains encircles me, they pierce my hands and my feet ... They divide my clothes among them and cast lots for my garment' (vs 7,8,16,18).

Read: Matthew 27:32–44

> What is the worst physical pain you have been in? Perhaps you have given birth, or you suffer from migraines, or you've torn a ligament or broken a bone... Crucifixion was designed to maximise the pain of the victim. Even with our own experiences of pain, it is hard to begin to imagine what Jesus underwent that day.
> Jesus could have come down from that cross at any moment he chose. What held him there?

Reflect on these words from Colossians 2: 'God ... forgave us all our sins, having cancelled the charge of our legal indebtedness, which stood against us and condemned us; he has taken it away, nailing it to the cross.' (vs 13,14).

32 As they were going out, they met a man from Cyrene, named
Simon, and they forced him to carry the cross. 33 They came to a
place called Golgotha (which means 'the place of the skull').
34 There they offered Jesus wine to drink, mixed with gall; but after
tasting it, he refused to drink it. 35 When they had crucified him, they
divided up his clothes by casting lots. 36 And sitting down, they kept
watch over him there. 37 Above his head they placed the written
charge against him: THIS IS JESUS, THE KING OF THE JEWS.
38 Two rebels were crucified with him, one on his right and one on
his left. 39 Those who passed by hurled insults at him, shaking their
heads 40 and saying, 'You who are going to destroy the temple and
build it in three days, save yourself! Come down from the cross, if
you are the Son of God!' 41 In the same way the chief priests, the
teachers of the law and the elders mocked him. 42 'He saved others,'
they said, 'but he can't save himself! He's the king of Israel! Let him
come down now from the cross, and we will believe in him. 43 He
trusts in God. Let God rescue him now if he wants him, for he said,
"I am the Son of God."' 44 In the same way the rebels who were
crucified with him also heaped insults on him.

Matthew 27:32–44

Time of death

'And when Jesus had cried out again in a loud voice, he gave up his spirit.'
Matthew 27:50

Read: Matthew 27:45–56

When someone we love dies, our world is not the same. But it continues on unchanged to those around us. Jesus' death was so momentous that the whole earth shuddered (v 51). What was going on? Why was his last breath so significant? How has his death changed things for *you*?

> When Jesus cries out in verse 46 (quoting Psalm 22), he doesn't just feel forsaken; he *has been* forsaken. On the cross, he was absorbing the weight of the world's sin, our sin included, separating him from the Father. More than the physical ordeal, this was the true cost of his sacrifice.
> The curtain in the Temple hung across the entrance to the inner sanctuary, and it ripped from top to bottom as Jesus died. From that moment on, God's people have free and direct access to his holy presence: MIND-BLOWING!
> We don't know much about the people who came out of their tombs, but we do know that Matthew included them in his account for a reason: Jesus' death means new life.

'Posterity will serve him; future generations will be told about the Lord. They will proclaim his righteousness, declaring to a people yet unborn: He has done it!' (Psalm 22:30,31).

[45] From noon until three in the afternoon darkness came over
all the land. [46] About three in the afternoon Jesus cried out in a loud
voice, *'Eli, Eli, lema sabachthani?'* (which means 'My God, my God,
why have you forsaken me?').
[47] When some of those standing there heard this, they said, 'He's
calling Elijah.'
[48] Immediately one of them ran and got a sponge. He filled it with
wine vinegar, put it on a staff, and offered it to Jesus to drink. [49] The
rest said, 'Now leave him alone. Let's see if Elijah comes to save him.'
[50] And when Jesus had cried out again in a loud voice, he gave up
his spirit.
[51] At that moment the curtain of the temple was torn in two from top
to bottom. The earth shook, the rocks split [52] and the tombs broke
open. The bodies of many holy people who had died were raised to
life. [53] They came out of the tombs after Jesus' resurrection and went
into the holy city and appeared to many people.
[54] When the centurion and those with him who were guarding Jesus
saw the earthquake and all that had happened, they were terrified,
and exclaimed, 'Surely he was the Son of God!'
[55] Many women were there, watching from a distance. They had
followed Jesus from Galilee to care for his needs. [56] Among them
were Mary Magdalene, Mary the mother of James and Joseph, and
the mother of Zebedee's sons.

Matthew 27:45–56

Dead and buried

'Joseph took the body, wrapped it in a clean linen cloth, and placed it in his own new tomb that he had cut out of the rock.'
Matthew 27:59,60a

The central principle of Christianity is that Jesus Christ died and was resurrected from the dead. From early on, people did their best to find other explanations for what happened – perhaps he did not quite die, or maybe grave robbers took the body, or the women returned to the wrong tomb. Matthew includes all sorts of details as evidence to support the claim that Jesus really did die.

Read: Matthew 27:57–61

> Would a Roman governor have risked releasing the body of a condemned rebel leader if he wasn't sure he was dead?
> In Palestine at the time, bodies were wrapped in cloth with spices and left to decompose. Sometimes several bodies shared a cave. When only bones were left, these would be placed in an 'ossuary' box. As this was a new tomb, Jesus' body was the only one there.
> Since grave-robbery was common, stones were used to provide a measure of security. These could not be removed without a great deal of effort.
> The two Marys were present throughout, and knew exactly which tomb he was in.

Ask God to help you believe history as Matthew wrote it.

[57] As evening approached, there came a rich man from
Arimathea, named Joseph, who had himself become a disciple
of Jesus. [58] Going to Pilate, he asked for Jesus' body, and Pilate
ordered that it be given to him. [59] Joseph took the body, wrapped it
in a clean linen cloth, [60] and placed it in his own new tomb that he
had cut out of the rock. He rolled a big stone in front of the entrance
to the tomb and went away. [61] Mary Magdalene and the other Mary
were sitting there opposite the tomb.

Matthew 27:57–61

Just to be sure

'"Sir," they said, "we remember that while he was still alive that deceiver said, 'After three days I will rise again.' So give the order for the tomb to be made secure until the third day."'
Matthew 27:63,64a

There are two groups of people particularly anxious to make sure that the tomb is well guarded and that Jesus stays dead – the Romans and the religious leaders. Their extra caution in sealing and guarding the tomb ended up backfiring on them however. They made it incredibly hard to explain the disappearance of the body.

Read: Matthew 27:62–66

> Do you believe that Jesus really died and that his body was secure in the tomb? Think carefully about the alternative theories. Are you happy with the evidence that refutes them?
> Use the journal space to write a summary of your current beliefs around the events of the past few days. Would you be confident to argue your position with a sceptic?

'Thank you that you died, as we all must, and for the hope that your death brings us, because it was not the end.'

[62] The next day, the one after Preparation Day, the chief priests
and the Pharisees went to Pilate. [63] 'Sir,' they said, 'we remember
that while he was still alive that deceiver said, "After three days I will
rise again." [64] So give the order for the tomb to be made secure until
the third day. Otherwise, his disciples may come and steal the body
and tell the people that he has been raised from the dead. This last
deception will be worse than the first.'
[65] 'Take a guard,' Pilate answered. 'Go, make the tomb as secure
as you know how.' [66] So they went and made the tomb secure by
putting a seal on the stone and posting the guard.

Matthew 27:62–66

Alive!

'The angel said to the women, "Do not be afraid, for I know that you are looking for Jesus, who was crucified. He is not here, he has risen, just as he said."'
Matthew 28:5,6a

If you were one of the Marys, you were about to have the best, and probably the most frightening, experience of your life...

Read: Matthew 28:1–10

> Although Jesus had predicted his resurrection on the third day, rationality had taken over and no one expected to see him again in the flesh. Mark and Luke tell us the women were bringing spices, hoping to complete the appropriate burial ritual.
> The reveal of the empty tomb is suitably dramatic: an earthquake, a blindingly bright angel, the rolling away of the stone, the guards in shock and terror. Imagine how you might have felt if you had been there.
> And then... Jesus himself – a risen Jesus, full of life – a Jesus still alive who we can know NOW, through the Holy Spirit, and who one day we will see face to face.

'If you declare with your mouth, "Jesus is Lord" and believe in your heart that God raised him from the dead, you will be saved' (Romans 10:9). Take any doubts to God and ask him to help you believe.

After the Sabbath, at dawn on the first day of the week, Mary
Magdalene and the other Mary went to look at the tomb.
2 There was a violent earthquake, for an angel of the Lord came
down from heaven and, going to the tomb, rolled back the stone
and sat on it. 3 His appearance was like lightning, and his clothes
were white as snow. 4 The guards were so afraid of him that they
shook and became like dead men.
5 The angel said to the women, 'Do not be afraid, for I know that
you are looking for Jesus, who was crucified. 6 He is not here; he has
risen, just as he said. Come and see the place where he lay. 7 Then
go quickly and tell his disciples: "He has risen from the dead and
is going ahead of you into Galilee. There you will see him." Now I
have told you.'
8 So the women hurried away from the tomb, afraid yet filled
with joy, and ran to tell his disciples. 9 Suddenly Jesus met them.
'Greetings,' he said. They came to him, clasped his feet and
worshipped him. 10 Then Jesus said to them, 'Do not be afraid. Go
and tell my brothers to go to Galilee; there they will see me.'

Matthew 28:1–10

Now but not yet

"... go and make disciples of all nations, baptising them ... and teaching them to obey everything I have commanded you."
Matthew 28:19,20a

Have you ever had to hold the fort while the person in charge was away? Chances are, they left you instructions and gave you advice before they left. But they couldn't have promised to be there with you after they had left. Jesus gives his crew of friends massive responsibility, but he doesn't abandon them to get on with it alone.

Read: Matthew 28:16–20

> Jesus' kingdom is here, and he's in charge (v 18). And yet, it has not come in its fullest sense, so there is work to be done, and he delegates this work to his followers. How amazing that we should have a role in bringing God's kingdom to its fullness!

> Have you been baptised? If so, what did it mean to you? If not, is it something you would consider?

Matthew's Gospel concludes with Jesus' promise that he will be with us always. Do you take him at his word? Pray now with faith that he is alive and with you now.

16 Then the eleven disciples went to Galilee, to the mountain
where Jesus had told them to go. 17 When they saw him, they
worshipped him; but some doubted. 18 Then Jesus came to them
and said, 'All authority in heaven and on earth has been given to
me. 19 Therefore go and make disciples of all nations, baptising
them in the name of the Father and of the Son and of the Holy Spirit,
20 and teaching them to obey everything I have commanded you.
And surely I am with you always, to the very end of the age.'

Matthew 28:16–20

"And surely I am with you always,
to the very end of the age."
Matthew 28:20

What is a Christian?

The word 'Christian' means follower of Christ, and 'Christ' is a Greek translation of the Hebrew word, 'Messiah'. Christians are those who believe Jesus to be the Messiah spoken of in the Old Testament: a king whose reign will last for ever, a Saviour bringing salvation to God's people, a 'suffering servant' whose suffering atones for the sins of the whole world.

The Christian narrative begins with the creation of the world from nothing. God spoke and it came to be and it was good. But from the beginning there was evil, in the form of a tempter sometimes known as Satan. The very first humans succumbed to temptation, wanting to be God-like in their knowledge of good and evil, and from that moment their close relationship with their Creator was damaged. Sin had come into the picture, and sin separated them and their descendants from a holy God. Romans 3:23 says 'all have sinned and fall short of the glory of God.'

But God loved his world, and was not about to abandon it to the fate it deserved – destruction. The great rescue plan was that God himself, born as a man, would pay the penalty. Jesus, both God and human, was an acceptable, sinless, perfect sacrifice and he willingly went to the cross to fulfil justice. The next verses in Romans go on to say, 'all are justified freely by his grace through the redemption that came by Christ Jesus. God presented Christ as a sacrifice of atonement, through the shedding of his blood – to be received by faith' (Romans 3:24,25a).

What Jesus did by dying in our place was to give us free access to God's presence, with no fear of judgement. But we are only there because of what he did, and we need to accept and receive that gift. We need to acknowledge that our relationship with God is broken through our sin, and that we need forgiveness and grace to mend things. We have a choice to make, because God doesn't force himself on anyone, and he will allow us to walk away if that is what we want.

Of course, accepting what Jesus has done for us is only the first step in an epic journey of transformation. The Bible speaks of the change as being as dramatic as rebirth, as beginning a new life, a life that will go on into eternity. If you have not yet begun that adventure, what is stopping you? There's no time like the present...

What next?

The Bible is alive. It contains the most powerful force in the universe: the Word of God. It's amazing but true that continuing to read the Bible regularly and expecting God by his Holy Spirit to speak through it can empower us all to live more like Jesus and to do the things he did.

Closer to God is published every three months, helping people around the world to meet God through reading the Bible and prayer. It is designed to provide a pattern for your time with God. As you listen to God each day, you'll get to know him better and learn to respond to him in love and obedience.

In *Closer to God* every quarter, you'll find:
> **Three months' worth of daily Bible readings** with notes and ideas to help you reflect, think and grow in your relationship with God. Each Bible book series lasts one or two weeks. As you use *Closer to God*, these form part of a comprehensive exploration of the Bible.
> **Images and journal spaces** – to help you reflect and jot down thoughts, ideas and prayers as part of your conversation with God.
> **A Bible in a year** plan which can be started at any time.
> **Articles**, poems and meditations to help you go deeper and look outwards.

Closer to God is available in both print and electronic formats, and you can save time and money by subscribing.

For a great offer
on an annual
subscription,
see page 95!

"He has risen, just as he said ..."
Matthew 28:6

Scripture Union produces three printed Bible reading guides: **Closer to God**, **Daily Bread** and **Encounter with God** – all helping you meet God daily through the Bible and prayer, but in different ways and styles. £3.99 each, quarterly.

You can also read the Bible online at **www.WordLive.org** with your choice of *Classic* notes, multimedia *Alt* resources and contemplative *Lectio* readings.

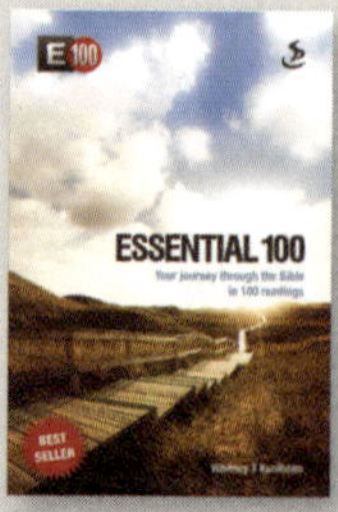

The **Essential** series is great for those who are new to Bible reading. **Essential 100** takes you through the big story of the Bible, and **Essential Jesus** reflects on who Jesus is in the light of both the Old and New Testaments. Why not read through them with a group of friends? £6.99 each.

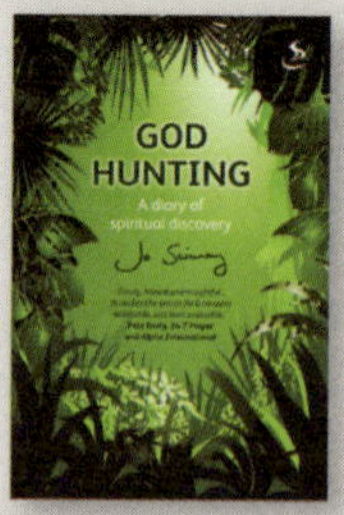

Also by author Jo Swinney, **God Hunting** takes you on a journey of discovery, searching for God through old and new spiritual disciplines. £6.99

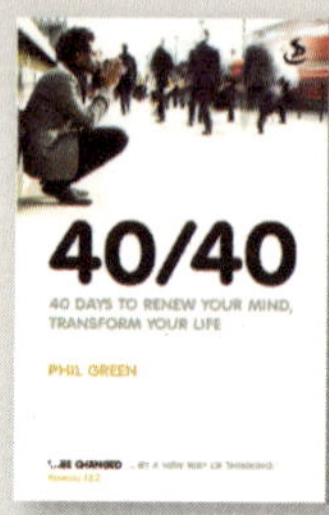

40/40 aims to renew your mind with 40 days of Bible readings and reflections for the morning and evening, getting into rhythms that help you meet with God as part of your everyday life. £5.99

All these books are available in both print and electronic versions.

To order:

- Visit **www.scriptureunion.org.uk/closertogodoffer**
- Phone **01908 856006**
- Use the **mail order** form opposite

Subscribe to Closer to God

And get your first issue FREE!

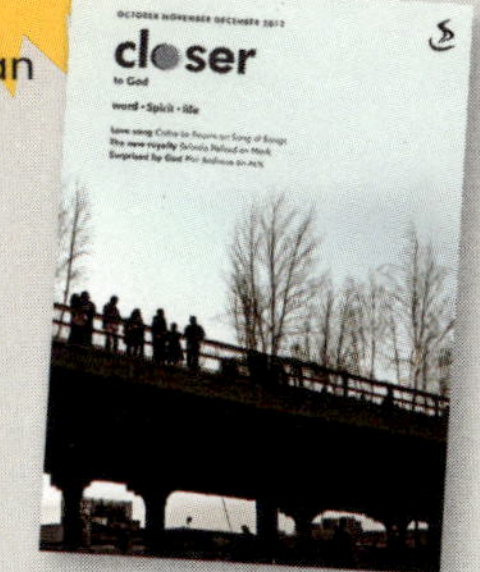

If you would like to continue reading *Closer to God*, why not take out an annual subscription and get it delivered to your door every quarter? If you subscribe now, you will get your first issue completely free!

To take up this offer:

- Go online to **www.scriptureunion.org.uk/closertogodoffer**
- Phone Scripture Union mail order on **01908 856006**
- Use the order form overleaf and send it to Scripture Union **by post**
- Take this order form to your **local Christian bookshop**

I would also like to order the resources featured in this issue.

Title	Qty	Price	Total
		Subtotal	£
		P&P (see below)	£
		Total	£

Please enter the total price of your order in the 'Order total' section on the form overleaf.

Postage and packing costs

Order value	UK	Europe	Rest of world
Under £7.00	£1.50	£2.50	£3.50
£7.00 to £11.99	£2.50	£3.75	£5.50
£12.00 to £24.99	Free	£5.00	£7.50
£25 and over	Free	20% of order value	30% of order value

Order form

I would like to take out an annual subscription to *Closer to God*, starting from the issue beginning in:

☐ Jan ☐ Apr ☐ Jul ☐ Oct

Name (Mr/Mrs/Miss/Rev)

Address

Postcode

Daytime tel

Email

Quantity ☐ UK ~~£15.00~~ £11.00 ☐ Europe ~~£20.00~~ £15.00
☐ Rest of world ~~£23.00~~ £17.25

To pay by direct debit, please phone 01908 856006
or tick here to be sent a form ☐

Subscription £

Additional items (see overleaf) £

Order total £ (see overleaf)

I enclose total payment of £ (in £ sterling only) by:

☐ Postal order ☐ Cheque payable to Scripture Union

Please debit my credit/debit card

Card No:

Cardholder's name

Expiry date: Issue No/Valid from:

Security No:

Cardholder's signature

Date

Subscriptions and book orders are available:

- ☐ **by phone:** 01908 856 006 ☐ **by fax:** 01908 856020
- ☐ **online:** www.scriptureunion.org.uk/shop
- ☐ **by post:** Scripture Union Mail Order, PO Box 5148, Milton Keynes MLO, MK2 2YX
- ☐ through your local **Christian bookshop**
- ☐ through your church **Bible reading representative**

We would like to keep in touch with you by placing you on our mailing list. If you would prefer not, please tick the box. Scripture Union does not sell or lease its mailing list. ☐

To the retailer: This coupon will be redeemed by Scripture Union on Bible-reading guide subscription orders only, provided it has been used for this offer and returned fully completed to Marston, Christian Customer Services Department, Unit 160 Milton Park, Abingdon, Oxon, OX14 4SD. *CTGN*